Michael,
   All the.

Jerry

# We're all CRAZY

## GET USED TO IT!

Jerold Skolnik

Copyright © 2021 Jerold Skolnik.

All rights reserved. No part of this book may be used or reproduced by any means, graphic, electronic, or mechanical, including photocopying, recording, taping or by any information storage retrieval system without the written permission of the author except in the case of brief quotations embodied in critical articles and reviews.

Balboa Press books may be ordered through booksellers or by contacting:

Balboa Press
A Division of Hay House
1663 Liberty Drive
Bloomington, IN 47403
www.balboapress.com
844-682-1282

Because of the dynamic nature of the Internet, any web addresses or links contained in this book may have changed since publication and may no longer be valid. The views expressed in this work are solely those of the author and do not necessarily reflect the views of the publisher, and the publisher hereby disclaims any responsibility for them.

The author of this book does not dispense medical advice or prescribe the use of any technique as a form of treatment for physical, emotional, or medical problems without the advice of a physician, either directly or indirectly. The intent of the author is only to offer information of a general nature to help you in your quest for emotional and spiritual well-being. In the event you use any of the information in this book for yourself, which is your constitutional right, the author and the publisher assume no responsibility for your actions.

Any people depicted in stock imagery provided by Getty Images are models, and such images are being used for illustrative purposes only. Certain stock imagery © Getty Images.

Print information available on the last page.

ISBN: 978-1-6698-2500-5 (sc)
ISBN: 978-1-6698-2501-2 (e)

Balboa Press rev. date: 12/02/2021

# CONTENTS

| | | |
|---|---|---|
| Chapter 1 | You Must Be Nice To Yourself | 1 |
| Chapter 2 | Everybody has a right to their own opinion | 3 |
| Chapter 3 | You are taking risks whether you think you are or not | 5 |
| Chapter 4 | Watch Your Choice of Words | 7 |
| Chapter 5 | Time For Us to Believe in Ourselves | 9 |
| Chapter 6 | We Are All Creatures of Habit | 11 |
| Chapter 7 | Nobody is Perfect | 13 |
| Chapter 8 | Limiting Beliefs | 15 |
| Chapter 9 | Your parents job was to keep you safe | 17 |
| Chapter 10 | Our convoluted ideas about money | 19 |
| Chapter 11 | Helping People | 21 |
| Chapter 12 | The Gift of Music | 23 |
| Chapter 13 | There is an Opposite to Everything | 25 |
| Chapter 14 | Welcome Change into your life | 27 |
| Chapter 15 | Paradigms | 29 |
| Chapter 16 | How important is it that others agree with you or that others like you? | 31 |
| Chapter 17 | There will always be some rough times | 35 |
| Chapter 18 | We experience good and bad days | 37 |
| Chapter 19 | Negativism reigns supreme | 39 |
| Chapter 20 | Compliments and Criticisms | 41 |
| Chapter 21 | We are what we think about. | 43 |
| Chapter 22 | We all receive gifts. | 45 |

| | | |
|---|---|---|
| Chapter 23 | What's holding you back? | 47 |
| Chapter 24 | Positive Vibes | 49 |
| Chapter 25 | Never Feel That You're Alone | 51 |
| Chapter 26 | World's Rapid Change | 55 |
| Chapter 27 | Take responsibility for your life | 57 |
| Chapter 28 | Rid yourself of doubts through affirmations | 59 |
| Chapter 29 | Think highly of yourself | 61 |
| Chapter 30 | It's your right to have abundance | 63 |
| Chapter 31 | Make a decision that you're going to become the person that you want to be | 67 |
| Chapter 32 | Perseverance | 71 |
| Chapter 33 | Don't be so sensitive | 75 |
| Chapter 34 | Let your little child out every once in a while | 77 |
| Chapter 35 | Learn New Things | 79 |
| Chapter 36 | Practice Spontaneity | 81 |
| Chapter 37 | Relationships | 83 |
| Chapter 38 | Your Money Story | 87 |
| Chapter 39 | How we view our loved ones | 91 |
| Chapter 40 | Think Like a Winner | 95 |
| Chapter 41 | Just be Yourself | 105 |
| Chapter 42 | Some Great Quotes | 109 |
| Chapter 43 | Mindset is Everything | 111 |

# CHAPTER 1

# YOU MUST BE NICE TO YOURSELF

First things first. You must be nice to yourself. We are our own worst critics. This needs to stop immediately. There is no perfect, and that includes all. Tell your bad thoughts to come back another time. Make sure that you never have time for them. Talk nicely to yourself. You are unique and you are a special person with God given talents. Utilize those talents starting now.

It is time to dwell on what you're good at and forget for a while what you're not so good at. Always speak nicely to yourself. Never berate yourself. How do you feel after you tell yourself off? I'm sure it is not too good. Go to the nearest mirror and look at your face after you just berated yourself. Now put a smile on your face and you will find that your nastiness to yourself has dissipated. You will probably start to laugh.

Always watch your words. You can't feel bad when you use good ones and you can't feel good when you use bad ones. Practice this on yourself and then use this method on others.

## CHAPTER 2

# EVERYBODY HAS A RIGHT TO THEIR OWN OPINION

Everybody has a right to their own opinion. You cannot expect all others to share the same opinion as you. There does not have to be a right or a wrong to everything. A fact is arguable but an opinion is not. Don't get riled up over the opinion of someone else.

Trust yourself. You are the only one who truly knows what you really feel. It doesn't matter if it is a parent, sibling, or best friend. You can ask if you want but you need to go with your gut feeling. That is the true answer as to what needs to be done.

## CHAPTER 3

# YOU ARE TAKING RISKS WHETHER YOU THINK YOU ARE OR NOT

Just remember that you are taking risks whether you think you are or not. That is why it is better to go with your gut. Do you really want to blame someone else if things don't go right?

That is the cowardly way out. Stand up straight with your head held high and take responsibility for your actions.

## CHAPTER 4

# WATCH YOUR CHOICE OF WORDS

Watch your choice of words especially when you're upset. We all have said things that we're not proud of when we're upset. You can use the mirror method if you need to. Just smile and then rethink what you were going to say.

Getting back to risk taking, we never know how things are going to turn out but you need to have the faith that they will turn out well. And even if they don't, now you know what didn't work which means you now have the chance to see what will work. Think of Thomas Edison. He failed hundreds and hundreds of times before he invented the light bulb. When asked as to why he didn't give up, he simply stated that he just found out another way how not to invent it.

Thomas Edison believed in his mind that he will figure this out regardless of how long it took.

## CHAPTER 5

# TIME FOR US TO BELIEVE IN OURSELVES

Isn't it time for us to believe in ourselves the same way that Edison believed in himself? Imagine what you could accomplish if you knew you couldn't fail Every single one of us has an Edison type idea buried in our brains. So what if people think you're crazy. The crazier the idea, the more ridicule you will have to endure. Do you think the Wright Brothers were ridiculed for having the audacity to believe that they could get a plane off the ground? It is time to develop a thick skin and to not care how much you might be laughed at when your idea gets out there.

What is more important? Is it your sensitivity issues or is it your brilliant idea that might help millions of people?

Let's go back to when you were a little child. Were you constantly chastised or were you always given a pat on the back? Were you allowed to voice your opinion or were you always told to be quiet? I'm sure of one thing. When you tried to take your first steps, I'm sure you were encouraged to do so. I've always wondered why there is not that sort of ongoing encouragement in other parts of growing up.

Think about it. The parent and the child are on the same page. The parent is going to want to tell the whole world that their child just began to walk. In the meantime, the child has no idea what it means to fail. Therefore, the child will continue to get up as many times as it takes until he or she succeeds. It's the best of both worlds. As long as the child is physically able to walk, it will eventually begin to walk. The bottom line here is that there will be no criticism or ridicule involved while the child continues to fall and get back up until the child succeeds.

For the parents who continue to encourage their children to persevere through the constant struggle called life, chances are that said child will grow up to be much healthier than the child who is constantly berated and ridiculed. Even when the encouraged child begins to go to school and encounters ridicule from fellow students, that child will be better equipped to handle such adversity.

Now let's get to competitive sports. The children that are encouraged are more apt to handle failure. How many times have we seen the parent who is living out his or her sports fantasy through their child? They scream at the game official and they have a tendency to scold the child if he or she does poorly. Some of them even tell their child to trip an opponent or kick them on purpose when the child on the other team is down. I've seen this. I know it occurs.

## CHAPTER 6

# WE ARE ALL CREATURES OF HABIT

We are all creatures of habit. What we learn while growing up stays with us unless we make the changes that need to be made so that we can all treat others the way we want to be treated.

When I say that, let's not forget that we are all different. However, what I basically mean is that we all want to be treated with a modicum of respect. Although our opinions differ, we still want our own opinion to be valued.

## CHAPTER 7

# NOBODY IS PERFECT

Nobody is perfect. If any of us were, life would be fairly boring. With that said, it is always my hope that most of us try to improve many facets of our life on a daily basis.

One of the ways to improve is to work on your self-image. Basically, your self-image is how you perceive yourself. What do you see when you look in the mirror? Do you like what you see?

Do you see a positive person or a negative one? Do you view yourself as attractive? Are you intelligent? Before you answer any of these questions, you must remember that you will most likely be perceived by others in the same way as you perceive yourself. If you have good posture, dress well and receive others with confidence, the persona that you present will be returned to you in kind.

If you don't like what you see, it is time to go about improving your self-image. This is not an easy task but it can be done without going to an expensive therapist. First of all, go back and look in that mirror. Stand up straight and put on a smile. Think about how you would feel when you meet someone new with that same posture and a genuine smile. Go to the nearest book store and get to the section with self-help books. Look specifically for books on the thing or things that are holding you back from having a better self-image.

Now comes the most important part. Read these books over and over and over again until you feel that you have conquered your fear or your limiting beliefs.

## CHAPTER 8

# LIMITING BELIEFS

All of our limiting beliefs are a result of the information that has been planted into our subconscious minds in our formative years. How many times have you met someone who is struggling financially and you just can't believe it. He or she is an absolute genius who should be making millions. Yet that same person is barely making ends meet. I read about one of these individuals. He was an enigma to all he came across. He was never able to make more than thirty thousand dollars in a year. A relative who saw his hidden potential paid to send him for counseling. After multiple sessions, it had been discovered that he had been yelled at by his father for some silly transgression. His father also stated that he would never make more than thirty thousand dollars a year. This particular man began to flourish and ended up making six to seven figures per year.

We are no different than a computer. What we are fed is what we believe. Our subconscious mind has no capacity whatsoever to distinguish right from wrong. Only your conscious mind can do that.

## CHAPTER 9

# YOUR PARENTS JOB WAS TO KEEP YOU SAFE

Your parents job was to keep you safe at all costs. Unfortunately, there were times when there were mixed signals and the stories that we heard stopped us from doing things that would ordinarily be deemed harmless. For instance, a friend of mine was told by her mother at a very young age that she should not go to the most popular amusement park in the state that she was living in at the time. As it turned out, neither she nor the rest of her siblings ever stepped foot in this park. There had been a bad accident in this said park and as a result, these children missed out on a lot of fun.

What we learn until the age of six stays in our subconscious and even though we're now adults, all that useless information is still in there. You must remember that much of this useless info was put there by our parents because it was their job to keep us safe.

Even when it came to their money thoughts for us, the bottom line is that they were trying to keep us safe. We must also remember that our parents ALSO have information that was stored in their subconscious minds by their parents and here is where it really gets tricky. Our grandparents' ideas on the meaning of money had to be vastly different from that which is stored in our minds. This is why we have got to create a new money story for ourselves if our current one is out of whack.

The way to do this is to inundate yourself with as many books on money and information on current programs that didn't exist over fifty years ago. How confident or right do you think you are when it comes to money? Do you trust the thoughts of your own parents or your spouse? Do you have a really good accountant and financial advisor? Don't leave your financial decisions to others. Get involved. It is critical to your financial wellbeing.

# CHAPTER 10

# OUR CONVOLUTED IDEAS ABOUT MONEY

Just to show you how convoluted our ideas are on money, I want to tell you a story of a public speaker who wanted to make a point and he sure did. He came out on stage and was dressed as if he were going to a millionaires' convention. He took a wad of cash out of his pocket and began to kiss it stating how much he loved money. As you would expect, the audience was horrified. He stood there for a few moments and then he addressed the audience. He asked them as to how would they have reacted if he had brought his two-year-old grandson out on stage and began to kiss him? After he received the applause about his grandson, the speaker waited a moment and then asked, What is wrong with loving money?

So, I ask you? what is wrong with loving money? The answer is that not only is there nothing wrong with it but I believe that you SHOULD love money. Why? Simply because the more money you have, the more people you can help. We all feel bad for anyone who is poverty stricken. I've read and tend to agree that it is our responsibility to become as wealthy as we can. We can then teach these poverty stricken people how to make money as opposed to just saying that we feel sorry for them. How great would you feel if instead of showering pity on those who are down on their luck, we get to help them instead.

Please don't misunderstand me. I'm not saying that we should become wealthy just to help the poor. What I am saying is that we should all accumulate as much money as we can so that we might be able to help others if the situation called for it. It would feel so much better to actually help a fellow human being as opposed to sending a charitable donation through the mail.

## CHAPTER 11

# HELPING PEOPLE

Now let's talk about just helping people in general, not just the ones who are financially challenged. Do yourself a big favor. Give positive vibrations to everyone that you meet. You will be amazed as to how much it will do for that person and just as importantly for you. Watch the looks on the faces of others when you smile and say Hi or when you compliment them in some way. When you do this with sincerity, it will make you feel just as good as the person you're conversing with. Keep the joking around to a minimum so that the person actually knows that you're being sincere. These exchanges can merely be a few seconds but they will go very far in helping to make someone's day.

I truly cannot believe the compliments that I'm getting on a daily basis since I've been doing this and these compliments that I'm receiving are not coming from the people that I compliment first. It just continues to prove that what you give out, you get back. Don't make the mistake in expecting something back from the person you helped or gave a gift to. But I guarantee you that that act of kindness will come back to you from somebody else.

One more note on gift giving. Always remember that when giving a gift, it is only a gift when you don't expect anything in return.

## CHAPTER 12

# THE GIFT OF MUSIC

Now that we've gotten on the subject of gifts, a great gift to give someone is their favorite music. If you don't know what type of music they like, it should not be too hard to find out. This type of gift will get you double brownie points. You went out of your way on two fronts. Not only did you find out what type of music they like, but you also are giving them a disc of their favorite group. Oh yes. A gift to be remembered.

What is your go to music or group? Better yet, do you have many types of music that you listen to? Music can become medicine to the soul. When you have one of those melancholy moments, music will become the elixir that you need at that moment. Whether it be jazz, rock, rap, or even opera, it can really help get you out of the doldrums that you might be in.

## CHAPTER 13

# THERE IS AN OPPOSITE TO EVERYTHING

We all must remember that there is an opposite to everything. Good and bad, salty and sweet, light and dark, fast and slow and on and on and on. What do you do when the negative ones start hitting you hard? There is good and bad to everything and not only that but the good and bad occurs every single day. It all depends on what your perception is or was about that particular day. I will never forget a particular day I had while selling hair salon products back on Long Island. I had had a very good day of selling but my last stop of the day did not go well and I let that one stop bother me for the rest of the night. Be a glass half full person and not the glass half empty one.

Along the lines of a glass that is half full or half empty, how would you compare Monday as opposed to Saturday or for that matter, a day of sunshine as opposed to a day of rain? I would venture a guess that Saturday and sunshine would certainly win that comparison. But why does a rainy day or a Monday have to be looked at that way? There are definitive advantages to rainy days or a Monday. For instance, a rainy day allows you to slow the pace a bit from the hustle and bustle of everyday life. It also is a big help to those of us who need rain to occur for the work that we do. Monday is an off day for so many people who work the entire weekend.

My point here is that we need to stop putting labels on things and enjoy every single day regardless of what that particular day brings. Put a positive spin on your life no matter what is going on. Tell your negative thoughts to come back tomorrow. You have no time for them today

## CHAPTER 14

# WELCOME CHANGE INTO YOUR LIFE

Welcome change into your life. Do something different today. Ride a bicycle for the first time in ten years. Shop at a store that you would never have walked in to before. Wear something different. Drive to a new town. We all have a tendency to do the same exact things day after day. Eventually, your shoulders will start to droop, your smile will vanish and worst of all, when you look at your significant other, you will get in a bad mood and you won't even know why. Do yourself a favor and try something new today. It will lift your spirits.

It is also a great way to help convert your mindset onto a different, and better frequency. This is imperative because while you continue to use your thoughts toward continued positive advancement, you will keep those pesky negative thoughts away from you. Your negative beliefs will continue to haunt you unless or until you make a concerted effort to rid yourself of them. These useless negative thoughts are known as paradigms. What are paradigms?

## CHAPTER 15
# PARADIGMS

Paradigms are a typical example or pattern of something. In other words, they are things that try to stop us from moving ahead to better ourselves. As I said earlier, when we were small children, we were extremely susceptible to any information that we were given. This info became our beliefs. Our subconscious minds took in all this information, and subconscious minds have no ability whatsoever to distinguish right from wrong. Therefore, as in the case of the $30,000 man, his subconscious mind told him that that was true.

Once these thoughts become buried in our subconscious minds, it is not easy to flush them out. It takes a lot of strenuous work to switch your paradigms. Extensive and expensive therapy is one way. The less expensive way is to feed your subconscious mind in the same way that you received the information in the first place. But, whereas when you were a little child, you only had to hear this once, now you have to use repetition through emotional words to change your paradigms. State your new phrases over and over with emotional feeling. Where do you get these new statements from? They come from books and the constant asking of questions to people in the know. Repetition is the only way to convince the subconscious mind to change these limiting beliefs. Read the books that you get over and over as well.

## CHAPTER 16

# HOW IMPORTANT IS IT THAT OTHERS AGREE WITH YOU OR THAT OTHERS LIKE YOU?

How important is it that others agree with you or that others like you? I have found that it is extremely important to most. I used to be one of those people but not so much anymore. As I have said, you are unique and so is everyone else. Your likes and dislikes are the ones that are the most important. You really have to take a look at how much credence you put in others determining which avenue you take in your decision making.

Terry Cole-Whittaker wrote a book called *What You Think Of Me Is None Of My Business*.

Now I know that that may sound harsh but that title makes a very valid point. You have no idea whatsoever as to what is going on in somebody else's mind and that includes your parents, or your spouse, or your siblings, or even your closest friend. You might think that you do, but you can never really know for sure. Don't let others steer you in the wrong direction.

For instance, let's use the example of losing weight. Your closest supporters could easily turn on you and not even consciously realize that they are doing so. As your weight begins to diminish, they start to see a new person in front of their very eyes. Some of your most staunchest supporters can be very uncomfortable with that and be afraid that you're no longer going to be the person you were before the weight was lost so they begin to sabotage you. This type of thing really does happen and as you can readily see, they had no intention of harming you.

Therefore, you must value your own opinion among all others. You can always listen as to what others have to say but make sure that the final decision is yours.

Change is inevitable whether you allow someone else to make your decisions or not. If you're an adult, you know exactly what I mean. All you have to do is look back on your life and you will see just how many changes you have gone through. If somebody had told me how my life would unfold when I was 16, I would have sent this person to the nearest mental asylum. I'm not saying this to complain, I'm simply saying that we never know what twists and turns life is going to throw our way.

My life was the total norm when it came to having a family. It's my professional career that has been unique. I spent the first thirty years in the gas station business, the next twenty years in the hair salon business and am presently a motivational speaker and author. How's that for a diversified career?

You always have to keep your eyes and ears opened for all kinds of opportunities. Do you think that Kurt Warner thought that he was going to become a Hall of Fame quarterback when he was working in a grocery store or even when he was playing in the Arena Football League? By the way he is the only player who is in the Hall Of Fame as an Arena and NFL player.

How many of you who are reading this book right now, can look back and say that they would have never believed how they have transitioned from one field to another? And isn't it these kinds of things that make life so interesting? Almost all of us have lived (even for a short time) in numerous places. When you look back at all these places, they all hold a special place for you even when it might not have been the happiest of times. We are a resilient bunch and tough times make you a stronger and better person if you let them.

## CHAPTER 17

# THERE WILL ALWAYS BE SOME ROUGH TIMES

There will always be some rough times but there will always be good times as well. Here are two examples of how certain things are looked at. A Hall of Fame baseball player fails to get a hit seven times out of ten. Who would ever think that that constitutes an elite player?

Many of us like to gamble. We go to Las Vegas. We head for the casino on cruise ships and elsewhere. Do we win more or do we lose more? These gorgeous looking hotels are not getting erected because we win more than we lose.

## CHAPTER 18

# WE EXPERIENCE GOOD AND BAD DAYS

We experience good and bad days on the very same day sometimes. I actually experienced one as recently as yesterday. In the morning, I took some medicine that made me feel worse than better. I then received a call back from Netflix while I was busy listening to an important webinar. End result: I was stuck on the phone with Netflix for way longer than I would have ever thought. At one point, I even started to laugh because they had me on my cell, my computer, and my television at the same time. As you could imagine, I was not very happy nor could I make up what I just said to you.

Fast forward to the afternoon after that trying morning. I went to Best Buy with my computer but with no appointment. I expected to be told that my appointment would be two weeks later. Instead, they took care of all three of my problems right away. So there it is: A morning that was not so good and an afternoon that was very good.

Win your day every day. That should be your goal. Get up every day and decide that today is going to be better than yesterday. I had no idea that my visit to Best Buy would turn out as well as it did. But I can tell you this: I did not allow my unfortunate morning to keep me in a foul mood. This allowed me to walk into Best Buy with a smile on my face, and when I asked for help in the nicest possible way, they were willing to help me even though I did not have an appointment. As I've always said, "You get a lot more with sugar than with spice."

The lesson to be learned here is that the attitude that you show to the person you encounter, will most likely result in the outcome you present to that person. Most of us can read the signals of others. This is why a smile is so incredibly powerful because when you smile, you're putting the other person at ease. There is no sense of conflict between two people when one or both are smiling.

## CHAPTER 19

# NEGATIVISM REIGNS SUPREME

Unfortunately, we live in a world where negativism reigns supreme. I'll give you two perfect examples. Have you ever seen this headline on the front page of the newspaper? "It's Going To Be A Beautiful Day Today." No, that will never happen because that headline will not sell. Ninety percent of the time, the headline is reserved for negative news because that is what does sell. The other example has happened to me on numerous occasions. I'll have dinner out and I enjoyed the food as well as the service. I will then ask the waiter or waitress to have the manager come to my table. The immediate response from said server is "Is Everything Okay? I reply "Yes". The manager starts heading over to my table with his or her head down and shoulders slouched. I say "I just wanted to let you know that this meal was great and that the service was great. The look on the face of the manager is incredible. He or she thanks me and doesn't know what to do for me to thank me. It is important to note that I only do this when it is warranted. I think it is important to point out a job well done by said restaurant.

## CHAPTER 20

# COMPLIMENTS AND CRITICISMS

On the subject of compliments, how do you feel when you get one? I've been getting a bunch of them lately and it really makes me feel good. Despite the fact that I'm very humble, I've learned how to accept compliments and they make me strive for more by continuing to help as many people as I can through my daily videos and the writing of this very book.

Take the time to compliment someone when you're out and about. They will know that you're being sincere just by the way that you're presenting the compliment. That person is not the only one who will feel good. You will feel just as good because you will know that you helped to make someone's day a little bit more special.

You can tell when you see someone who looks like they haven't smiled in a really, really long time. I find this to be so sad. These people have no idea that they can turn their lives around so easily. It is simply a matter of changing their mindset. Instead of thinking about the things that they should be thankful for, they dwell on what is wrong in their lives.

Our life can go south in a hurry. You don't like your

spouse. You hate your job. Your financial situation is not in good shape. Your children are not doing well in school. This hardship list can go on and on. All this can change in a heartbeat because once you change your thought pattern you can change your life around.

## CHAPTER 21

# WE ARE WHAT WE THINK ABOUT.

We are what we think about. When you continually concentrate on lack, that is exactly what you will get. Think abundance, and that is what you'll get. Take your spouse out. Do something that is fun with him or her. Put more care in your job and start thinking of another job that you might like. Sit down with your spouse and figure out your financial situation and figure out how you can improve it. Do some physical exercise and include your spouse and your children. As your attitude begins to improve, you'll notice everybody else's will as well. It will be infectious.

Attitude is everything. How you feel and how you think go hand in hand. We are what we think about. Pleasant thoughts send out positive vibes. Worrisome thoughts send out bad vibes. Have you ever noticed that when you are in the right zone, that everything is in harmony and things go amazingly well? Same goes the other way around. When things are not going well, everything seems to go in the wrong direction. That is why it is extremely important to set your brain on the right vibration and frequency so that it can send you in the right direction.

What you read, what you say, whatever signals your

body is showing to others, is the key to where you're going. Do you want to manifest good or bad into your life? The answer to that question does not need to be answered. Are you afraid of success? There is no need to be. You have as much right to be rich as anyone else as long as it's through the creative means and not the negative means.

As I've said before, the more riches that you accumulate, the easier it will be to help that many more people. Continue to show people how they can attain riches, and your bank account will grow. You can grow your company, hire more people and help spread correct information out there. Money is NOT the root of all evil. Money is NOT only for the already rich. There is enough money out there to get these great ideas you have to come to fruition. The time is now to make the world a better place. Use your platform to make it that way.

We must remember though that money alone will not make someone happy. There are multi-millionaires out there who are miserable. Yes, they have a lot of money but every other part of their lives are not working for them. If your body, mind, and soul are not fulfilled, chances are that no amount of money is going to make you happy. I'm not looking to name drop here but how many famous people can you name that took their own lives because they were unhappy

Don't forget to lose sight of what you're really after. The money that you earn has got to be used for the right reasons. Make sure that your mind is in the right place and that the money that you're earning is continuing to help you grow in all the other ways. Don't be one of these famous people that had millions of dollars but they couldn't live another day. I know that it seems that I'm going to negative town but there is a method to my madness.

## CHAPTER 22

# WE ALL RECEIVE GIFTS.

We all receive gifts. How many of yours have you opened? This is what I mean. When you were born, you received many gifts. I call them talents. Have you utilized your talents? As I've said before, we are all unique. Every single one of us have been given these talents. As far as I'm concerned, the most successful people are the ones who opened more of their gifts. Isn't it time that you opened more of yours?

I know what most of you are thinking. I wasn't given these gifts. I have so many inadequacies.

Unfortunately, we concentrate on the inadequacies and not the gifts. Isn't it time to turn this equation around? If I met with each of you individually, it would take me less than five minutes to present you with an assortment of gifts that you have received. You just haven't taken the time to think of what they are and how they can be utilized.

I'll use myself as an example. Up until recently, all I ever thought about were my inadequacies. I was never a good student and I thought that I was not smart. I was very immature, and I gave up very quickly if I didn't grasp something right away. Needless to say, I was lost when it came to algebra, geometry, and the like. I thought of myself as a failure. It wasn't until way later in life that I learned about the many different ways that we can learn. The way they teach in school was definitely not one of those ways for me.

I began to realize what my gifts were many years later. My love of sports, music, and the need to help people are just a few. After I was married and had children, my mother found some stories that I had written when I was eight years old. They were all about the cartoons that were on television at the time. Dick Tracy and Top Cat were always on. I read my stories and was amazed at how well I wrote. However, I was never encouraged by anyone to keep doing it. My knowledge of sports is off the charts. I remember things that nobody remembers. Many of my friends don't believe some of it so they look it up on their computers.

So what am I doing now? I'm writing a book, I'm going to be doing sports podcasts with a partner, and I'm doing motivational speaking. I spent thirty years in the gas station business and twenty years in the hair salon business. I did extremely well in both but never loved either one so I made the decision to do the things that I love and that is what I'm going to do. Isn't it time for you to do the thing or things that you love to do?

I totally understand that if you have a high paying job and you have young children, you can't just drop everything to explore your dreams. However, these dreams of yours have got to be thought of in your very near future. Begin to plan ahead and start thinking about how you're going to begin to implement a future plan to do what you were meant to do.

And for those of you whose children are out on their own and taking care of their own families, you can pursue your dreams right now. Walt Disney said: *"All our dreams can come true if we have the courage to pursue them."* He pursued his dream with Walt Disney World.

## CHAPTER 23

# WHAT'S HOLDING YOU BACK?

All that is holding you back are your doubts and your fears. Now is the time to conquer these doubts and fears. There are so many different ways to conquer these doubts and fears. First of all, you have to know what you really want. If that is indeed the case, you have the hardest part figured out. Next, you have to know that you are not alone in your pursuit. Once you get started, help will arise from all angles. I know that this last thing that I just said may sound crazy, but it is absolutely true. I totally had my doubts about this and I was proven wrong almost immediately. As soon as I decided as to what I wanted to do, I ran into people who knew someone who could help me and I didn't even ask for this help!

## CHAPTER 24

# POSITIVE VIBES

Your positive vibes attract this help to you. It really truly does. You have to see this to believe it. There are books and videos that you can watch on the topics that are your passion. These are also tools that can be utilized. Then there will be things that just come to your mind for you. For instance, I am doing a program this coming weekend. As opposed to being worried about how many people are going to show up, I simply reference my Tony Robbins story. Tony is the most famous of them all when it comes to public speaking. When he first got started, he invited one hundred or so people to his very first event. Only two people showed up. So for me, I'm not worried at all about how many people are going to show up to my event. The other thing that I have planted in my brain is this: I am so intent on helping people push through their fears and their negativity, I have told myself that even when a particular program I'm doing does not go well, I'm not going to let it bother me simply because I have to continue to help.

Your positive vibes can only be manifested if you change your rules for success. Here is a great example of rules for success. A number of years ago, there was a program that called for two men to come up on stage and state their rules for success. The first man said that you have to be making two million dollars a year and have 2% body fat. He stated that because of his rules for success, he was a failure. This man was making a million dollars a year and had 10% body fat. I think that we would all agree that this man was highly successful but he didn't think so and what a shame that is. The second man was also successful despite the fact that he wasn't a millionaire and needed to shed a few pounds. When asked as to whether or not he was successful, he said, "If I wake up in the morning and put me feet on the ground, I am a success.

Watch your posture. Watch your words. Watch your attitude, and most of all watch your thoughts. It means more than you could ever know. Visualize the new you. Think of what you want and not what you don't want.

I cannot stress how important it is to be positive on an ongoing basis. Positive breeds positive and negative breeds negative. I used to think that that was a bunch of malarkey. Believe me when I say that it is not. Stop reading or watching things that send out negative vibes. Divorce friends that bring you down or are always negative. Surround yourself with people that are upbeat and positive. You will see your life transform before your very eyes.

When the new you start to evolve, start to take some chances. Believe that you will succeed at whatever you try. Don't let your loved ones discourage you. There is no such thing as failure. All that failure is feedback. Now you know what doesn't work. Try something else that might work, and if the next thing doesn't work, try something else. Remember, Edison failed and failed until he invented the light bulb.

## CHAPTER 25

# NEVER FEEL THAT YOU'RE ALONE

Never feel that you're alone when things aren't working for you and you need to try something new. As long as you don't give up, the answers will appear for you to help you in areas or from people that you would never expect. We all make mistakes and these mistakes act as growth. Whether you did something wrong or said something wrong is not important going forward. What is important is that now you know what you should not have done which makes you on the way as to what needs to now be done. Do not beat yourself up over these mistakes. Instead feel proud that you know what you did wrong and allow yourself to move ahead with a clear mind. Once you master this skill, it will be easier for you to pursue your dreams.

Don't think for a second that your dreams are unattainable. Walt Disney was no different than you or me. Almost everyone would have sent him to the nearest asylum when he had his idea. How about Henry Ford? He was told that the car was an impossibility and he was told this over and over. He just kept sending his workers back into the shop and told them that no matter how long it takes; I will have my car. The Wright brothers were thought to be out of their minds when they flew the first plane which was in the air for about thirty seconds.

Do you think that your ideas are anywhere near as crazy as Ford or Disney? I doubt it. All I know is that your idea might help millions of people if it were to be implemented, not to mention the fact that it could make you into a multi-millionaire. So before you put your idea on the back burner, think really hard as to what you're leaving on the table.

Never give up too quickly. We've all heard the stories about the owners who sold their land to look for diamonds and right after they sold their land, diamonds upon diamonds were found on the property. There are many morals to that story but the one that I take from it is that right after a so called failure comes the equivalent of a giant success. You can't succeed without struggle. Every single solitary multi billionaire that is out there had numerous failures before they hit it big. Think of it this way. Would it be possible for any new business to get off the ground without having any problems along the way? You already know the answer to that. Always keep in mind that there is really no such thing as failure. Failure is simply feedback. What you tried to do did not work so there are numerous other ways to get the job done.

Think of a baseball team. A nine-man lineup gets put on the field. How many times does that lineup get changed throughout the course of a season? The answer is that it is changed almost daily. The manager decides on a daily basis as to what lineup might work for the game today. There are 162 games in the regular season. Even the best teams are going to lose at least fifty of those games. Players that are lucky enough to make it to the Hall Of Fame still only get a hit three times out of ten. That is absolutely crazy when you think about it.

The example I just gave is a perfect segue into never

allowing the word failure to enter your mind. The word should be removed from the dictionary because it no longer has any meaning. The only way that the word failure has any meaning anymore is to pair it with two other words Those two words would be Giving Up. Once you give up, you have indeed failed. On the flip side of that though, is that as long as you persevere and refuse to let the so called failure stop you, you will be on your way to possibly the biggest breakthrough of your entire life.

All the names have already been mentioned. Now it is time for you to step up and become the next Edison, Ford, Disney, or maybe pair up with your brother or sister like the Wright Brothers did. I haven't even mentioned Elon Musk. Look at what that guy has done and continues to do.

We are headed to the era of The Jetsons. I was only nine years old when that cartoon hit the television screens. Little space cars flying through the air. Meals fully prepared by just pushing a button. One day we will be on the west coast and will get a call inviting us to go to dinner on the east coast. We will get in our space car, push a button, go to sleep and arrive on the east coast in time for dinner. Maybe the dinner will get done by pushing a button, just like it was on the Jetsons cartoon which began in 1962.

There are so many new innovations that will be upon us. I believe that there will be a store like an Auto Parts that will be selling body parts that you just buy and attach with instructions. It is also only a matter of time before there is no such thing as cash or credit cards. You'll have a chip inserted in your hand that will be presented to the vendor and that chip will tell the vendor as to whether or not you can gain entry.

In the meantime, we are in 2021 and not in 2071 so what can we do right now to make our lives much better? The answer to that question is both simple and complicated.

We need to become the best possible version of ourselves so we can help make the entire world a better place. I made a video on Facebook yesterday that close to fifty people complimented me about. This video simply stated that if you want the best, you have to want the best for everyone. I do mean everyone. You heard that correctly. We attract what we think about. When you wish harm on people that you totally dislike, you're bringing that dislike right back to you. How many times have you heard the phrase: Karma is a b--ch? Guess what? It's not just a phrase. It's the truth!

## CHAPTER 26

# WORLD'S RAPID CHANGE

Now that we know that the world is changing so rapidly and that all these new innovations are upon us, my advice is to allow these changes into your life. I just had to purchase a new cell phone and I dreaded it because I knew that I would have to learn all the new things that come with the new phone. The end result was that despite the fact that it took me about three full days to figure out all the new features, the new phone is so much better. I knew it would be but I held off in getting it because I knew the next few days after I bought it would be a challenge.

It wasn't that long ago that there were no cell phones. Remember Blockbuster Video and VCR's? I remember the first time that I fast forwarded a commercial on television. I also remember the first television show that was televised in color.

We can find things out instantaneously now. I remember having to wait up until 11:20 in order to find out who won a particular game on that night. We can't even imagine what new things we are all going to encounter by 2025. It is going to be incredible. Welcome these changes. They will all be for the better.

In lieu of all these changes, take baby steps and don't do

anything drastic. Definitely take risks but don't be careless when doing so. Carefully plan your risk taking so you can change your plans if the original ones don't come to fruition. Plan your work and work your plan.

Look to improve every day in all your endeavors but don't be afraid to ask for advice or get opinions on what you plan to do. Always remember though that the final decision is yours.

## CHAPTER 27

# TAKE RESPONSIBILITY FOR YOUR LIFE

Take responsibility for your life. What I'm saying has nothing to do with selfishness. Remember this: You are always the problem and you're always the solution. I know that we all have our go to people who are always there for us but we're the ones who have to make the final decisions

We all think that we can't survive without our go to people but the bottom line is that those go to people are not us. You may think that you know what they're thinking but the bottom line is that you don't because that is impossible. Now I'm not saying that they are not trustworthy but I am saying that we are all individuals and we all have our own minds. Bottom line: Don't let anyone be the final decision maker besides you.

I'm not saying this to sound harsh. I'm simply saying that you need to be the one that is taking full responsibility for whatever it is that you're trying to do. Do you really want to blame others for a failed project? Believe me when I say you don't.

Flip this around and look at it this way. When your idea or project begins to flourish, do you really want others to be able to claim that it was their idea? Let me be perfectly clear. I'm not saying that your go to people have anything but your best interests at heart. What I am saying is that you're the one that needs to take full responsibility for what you're trying to accomplish

Don't let self-sabotage invade your mind. Don't have any self-doubt. You've come this far for a reason. You must believe that you were meant for this moment. This is your time to shine You have earned this. You are entitled to this success.

## CHAPTER 28

# RID YOURSELF OF DOUBTS THROUGH AFFIRMATIONS

If you do have any doubts, rid yourself of them through affirmations. Write them down and read them aloud constantly with emotion. This is the only way that they are going to find their way into your subconscious mind. Remember this important fact. Your subconscious mind has no capacity to differentiate right from wrong. Write down your affirmations and say them out loud until your subconscious mind accepts them as true statements.

In case you're having trouble coming up with affirmations, here are some examples:

- I always have a great self-image.
- I love what I see when I look in the mirror
- I achieve my definitive plans all the time.
- I am worthy of all great things.
- I always believe in myself.
- I have a great attitude
- I have a mindset of abundance.
- I think, feel, and act like a winner.

There are zillions of them. Formulate your own. Use words and phrases that work for you. Please remember to say them out loud and use emotion while doing so. If you live with others, don't let them discourage you. If you feel subconscious while doing it with other people around, simply go into another room and do it there or better yet, simply just don't care what they think while you're doing it. You're the beneficiary of this exercise, not them.

## CHAPTER 29

# THINK HIGHLY OF YOURSELF

I cannot stress enough as to how important it is for you to think highly of yourself. That is why these affirmations are so vitally important. It is about time that you value all of your attributes. Stop carrying on about what you're not good at and start concentrating on the things that you are good at. As unfortunate as it is to say this, I think we can all agree that negativism sells but optimism does not.

That is actually one of the first things to do when turning your life around. Stop being part of all this negativism. You can choose to not go there. Take all negative statements and news flashes and turn them in to a form of growth. Don't entertain or give any thought to the naysayers. Bring your mind into the positive world and tell your negative thoughts to get lost.

On that note, if you were asked to put together a list of all the people you love, would your name be on that list? If you said no, the list is meaningless. Why? Because if you can't love yourself, how are you going to love anyone else?

Your life can be so much better than it is if you make these switches. As the song says: *Don't Worry Be Happy*. Use optimism not pessimism, think abundance not lack, think of what you do want, not what you don't want, and most importantly, keep working toward your goals with a mindset that says: I always succeed at whatever I try to do. Setbacks only act as a means to tell me what doesn't work. Keep trying till what your after does work. Don't ever give up until the ultimate goal or goals have been achieved.

## CHAPTER 30

# IT'S YOUR RIGHT TO HAVE ABUNDANCE

It's your right to have abundance. It is also everybody else's right as well. Never let the words lack or poverty enter your mind. Instead of feeling sorry for others, become rich yourself and show the poverty stricken people the way to riches.

So many of you are probably saying that that is great advice but how do I get rich so I can show others how to get rich. Well, you start by first deciding that you are going to be rich. Affirmations books, mindset, and the faith and desire to do so. You don't need the genie in the bottle. The genie is already heredity is you. Simply decide that this is going to happen and nothing will stop you until it does. I'm not here to say that this is easy. We have all learned by now that life is not easy. It is not for the timid, it is not for the squeamish. It is for the go getters. You can do it. You truly can.

For those of you that are on the verge of going from couch potatoes to go getters, understand that the only thing stopping you from success is fear. There are too many to even mention but here are a few: Fear of Success, Fear of Failure, Fear of Ridicule, Fear of Your Inadequacies. You must not forget that everyone, and I mean everyone has fallen prey to one or more of these fears. You have to find a way to get past these fears. Take a risk. What do you have to lose?

Remember, whether you take a risk or not, you are because when you don't take a risk, you'll never, ever know what you could have accomplished. Do a little bit at a time. Take baby steps. That is what I'm doing by writing this book. I write a page or so a day. I'm not writing this whole book in one afternoon.

As you get started on your journey of doing what you want to do, you will find that help will come out of the woodwork to guide you in the right direction. You will never be alone in your quest for greatness. For me, it was a young woman who lives in New York. She pushed me to start doing daily videos. I fought it off as long as I could until one day when she said to me that I need to stop procrastinating and start doing the videos.

The first few were not very good but I had at least started and I didn't want my work to go to waste. What happened? They started to get better and better and now when I sit down to do them, I love it. I've become very good at it if I must say so myself. If it wasn't for this young girl who wouldn't let me off the hook, I doubt very highly that I would have ever started doing these videos. As a result of the daily videos, that I post on Facebook, I'm now writing this book. So you see, it is not only your best friends and loved ones that get you going, it could be a perfect stranger. This is why you should not only discuss your passions with those close to you. Don't be afraid to discuss them with perfect strangers and listen to what their passions are as well. The feeling that it gives you will be reciprocal. You just might help each other to achieve some of these goals and dreams.

When you start doing this on a regular basis, you

yourself will become unstoppable. What I mean by that, is with each person you chat with, your confidence will grow to astounding proportions. You will become more comfortable with the new you, and you will notice how easy it is to share your experiences with others while you learn all kinds of new things from them. There is never ending positivity in this sort of conversation.

You may end up with a new business partner. You can get a new idea that you never would have thought of in a million years. You might have a family member that can benefit from what the other person is doing and vice versa.

I am not suggesting that you approach anyone and immediately try to sell them something. Instead, what I'm saying is to just engage them in conversation and see if there is any commonality and just go on from there. There are only benefits to be gained when you start doing this. Of course not everyone is going to want to engage you in conversation but I can guarantee that more people will than won't as long as you engage them in a nice way.

Throw a compliment their way but be sincere because if you're not, chances are that they will see right through you. Your passion for what you're doing will begin to shine through.

As you can now see, you're now in the throes of changing your life from dealing with your weaknesses and concentrating on your strengths instead. Can you even imagine what that is going to be like? Things like anger, resentment, jealousy, and hatred will begin to melt away from your life. These emotions are so very unhealthy. I've lived these things, I know.

These unhealthy emotions can really do a number on your physical health. Back in 2012, my girlfriend broke up with me because I wasn't religious enough for her, yet we were the same religion. My managers boss sought me out and told me to stop losing weight.

When I think back to that time now, I smile and almost begin to laugh. It is so not who I am anymore. I learned the lesson that if someone doesn't want to be with you anymore, find somebody that does. It is really that simple but when your self-esteem is at a very low point, it is extremely difficult to see that. At this point in my life, I have almost rid myself of any negativity. You will be amazed at how happy you can be when you allow yourself that luxury.

CHAPTER 31

# MAKE A DECISION THAT YOU'RE GOING TO BECOME THE PERSON THAT YOU WANT TO BE

You simply have to make a decision that you're going to become the person that you want to be. But once you make that decision, you have to take the necessary steps to become that new you. I'm not going to kid you. This will not be easy. The program that you are currently in is not going to go away without a fight. Your original programming was designed with providing safety first. The new ideas are foreign to your subconscious mind. Constant repetition and new affirmations will work to get the job done. However, there are two things that you must remember. The original program will fight to stay. It will do whatever it can to sabotage the new program. You yourself will try to keep the old plan in place. Sounds crazy, right? But that is what is going to happen. It will not seem like a fair fight at first. You need to see that it is two against one. Your original programming along with your beliefs regarding the old programming, versus the new programming. Now you can see how difficult this is going to be.

Take solace in knowing that this changeover will not cause physical pain. Nobody is going to give you a painful shot in your abdomen. However, this change will not take place in a day or even in a week or month. You will have to work on this, every single day. Your new affirmations have to be said out loud with emotion. And they must be said many times per day. Make sure that you say them when you first wake up and right before going to sleep as well.

It took me about six months because I didn't believe my own affirmations. Until you truly believe that you really are the new you, you will stay stagnant. Start writing out your new affirmations today. Say them in front of a mirror if you need to. And don't let anyone deter you.

Stay away from the ones who have a major influence over you when it comes to what you want to do. I will give you a personal example. One of my best friends in New York has been a motivational speaker. I purposely have not spoken to him about what I'm doing because I know that he is going to tell me the downfalls of doing it and believe me when I say that he means no harm whatsoever. He would have that influence over me that I don't want to hear. So you see, I'm not talking about someone that is looking to hurt you. I'm simply talking about those who can easily persuade you to not go after your dream or dreams.

I had given you a good example before about someone who wants to lose weight. Some of those major influencers could easily sabotage the person who is intent on losing weight and not even realize that they are doing so. The major influencer might simply be afraid on a subconscious level that the person is going to change too much when they lose the weight and they don't want that to happen.

The point is that most of these major influencers have the best intentions. It's just that they're going to possibly hurt your chance of succeeding if you let them. Bottom line is that you need to be the one to go after what you want and don't let your fears get in the way. You might even seek out the opinions of the major influencer so that you don't have to face the fear of what you want to do. Please remember this: The hardest part of any new venture is the start. If you get up on stage, you can't do your twentieth show without doing your first. Do you think that your first show will be as good as your twentieth? Not very likely. But if you never try or never begin, you will never, ever know what could have been. Do you really want to take that chance? Remember this: Whether you take a risk or not, you are taking a risk. Try it. You can do it.

Change is inevitable but personal growth is a choice. It is all up to you. It took me years to figure out what I wanted to do to help people and I finally stopped making excuses and procrastinating. Please don't wait as long as I did. Utilize those talents and gifts that you were born with to make a difference in the world.

Are you one of the people like Edison, Ford, or Musk who have an idea that is really out there? An idea that can change the course of our lives? Don't be afraid to share these ideas. Yes, you will most likely be ridiculed for your outlandish idea. But look at it this way. If your idea comes to fruition, it will bring you a sense of satisfaction that will be off the charts.

It is a known fact that if someone wants something bad enough, and they never give up in their quest to attain it, they will eventually get it. Let's go over the success story of Sylvester Stallone.

He was an actor getting bit parts. He saw a boxing match between Chuck Wepner and Muhammed Alethic led to the story of Rocky. Stallone took the script to every director that he could find, many of them numerous times. He wasn't getting any positive feedback whatsoever. Finally, after a number of rejections that were too many to count, a director was willing to give it a try. He told Stallone that Rocky was going to be played by Ryan O'Neal. Sylvester walked out saying that he was Rocky. He ended up selling his wife's jewelry without her permission. He even sold his dog. He lost his wife but got his dog back by paying the new owner a reported $10,000 dollars and a bit part in the movie.

## CHAPTER 32
# PERSEVERANCE

His perseverance ended up as a huge win for him which you already know. It has even been said that all the guys that he killed in the Rambo movies were the directors that turned him down for the right to be Rocky in all the Rocky movies.

There are never ending stories of people who became famous because they would not take no for an answer. I know of a guy that mailed HIMSELF to a company so that they would give him a job. It worked and now the guy is making a fortune. I went to High School with him.

I'm now going to flip to the opposite side of the spectrum. If you're suffering from this insidious disease, you need to cure yourself of this immediately. You need to stop berating yourself. In other words, stop beating yourself up. We all know by now that we can be our worst enemy. We expect way too much of ourselves sometimes. Take a deep breath and look in the mirror. Now, forgive yourself for any silly error that you might have made in the last hour. Also, remind yourself that you are a human being and you're not infallible.

I try very hard not to say the wrong thing or do the wrong thing, but I no longer berate myself when I do. Look at it this way. You do way more right things than wrong things, and when you do make a mistake, you correct it. Guess what? That is really all that you can do. I can no longer live my life by watching every single action that I take or every single word that I say. That is no longer on my agenda. As long as you have good intentions every single day, no longer worry or stress about making a boo boo every once in a while.

There is no perfect. It just doesn't exist. I feel really bad about certain things that I've done or things that I've said. However, I was never malicious or mean spirited about it. Bottom line: It's just not worth it in the long run. Watch your words, think before you speak. You'll have trouble taking it back once you do. Think of it this way: How would you feel if somebody said to you what you're about to say. I don't think that anyone deep down wants to scar someone. Do you?

We all want to be loved and respected. We all want to be liked and appreciated. We also want to appreciate others for the good things that they have done for us. It seems to me though that the majority of us spend way more time complaining than we do appreciating.

I used to be as guilty of this as anyone. It's only recently that I spend as much time as possible feeling happy and grateful for the things that I do have and way less time thinking about the things that I don't have. There are people out there who don't have a place to live and don't have enough to eat. Almost every exit ramp has somebody at the end of it that is asking for help. I am well aware that a good number of these people are scammers. But what about the ones who are legitimate?

I'm not saying that we should all roll down our windows and shower these people with money. Instead, I propose a different solution, one that would benefit us as well as them. Make a concerted effort to make as much money as YOU can so you can have all the things that you want and show others how to make money so that they no longer need your help.

Just think of how rewarding it would be to show someone how to rebuild their life without you just handing money over to them. Don't think for a minute that you're raising someone's self-esteem by putting money in their hand. It will help them for a moment but it will only last for that moment. Do yourself a favor and become wealthy. You can help so many people when you do. You will help your family, friends, and others when you do. Your whole life will improve more than you could ever possibly imagine.

The first step in becoming rich is to have the belief that you can. Henry Ford once said that whether you think you can or you think you can't, you're right. Ford was right on target when he uttered that quote. The belief that you can be rich or that you will be rich comes from you and you alone. Work on your affirmations. Say them out loud. Rid yourself of your negative beliefs.

I'm not going to kid you. This takes time. Remember that you have been carrying around the negative beliefs in your subconscious mind for many years. You're going to have to dig deep to rid yourself of the things that no longer serve you. These negative thoughts hit you at the most inopportune times. The key is to recognize when they come about. I'm getting really good at recognizing mine. For instance, when I feel that I'm being ignored, instead of getting upset, I take a deep breath and say that that person isn't really ignoring me, they just have something else on their mind and I don't take it personally.

## CHAPTER 33

# DON'T BE SO SENSITIVE

Don't be so sensitive. It will set you back and stop you in your tracks from achieving your goals. Everyone has their own agenda. We can't expect people to know what we're thinking and I can pretty much guarantee you that we don't know what they're thinking. Give them the benefit of the doubt. Just go forward and do what you need to do to be on your way to wealth.

I used to drive myself crazy trying to figure out what my wife was thinking and it was even worse when I tried to figure out what a new girlfriend might be thinking. It is only now that I realize that it is a waste of my time and energy to try and figure these silly things out. I also never stopped to think that men and women process their thoughts in completely different ways. But that is a story for another day.

Let us now look at the young child that is still inside of us. What happened to that little child? Simply put, that child grew up and is now an adult. Whether we know it or not, that little child comes out in all kinds of different ways. Most of them are unacceptable to both ourselves and those around us. Just like everything else in life, we need to utilize the skills of our inner child.

Case in point: I have a two-year-old grandson who I get to see fairly often. I take out my cell phone and play songs for him. The main ones are *Twinkle, Twinkle Little Star, Old McDonald Had a Farm,* and *The Twelve Days of Christmas.* I look at him and he is mesmerized. Why is it that we never seem to be mesmerized by anything? It is because we have seemingly grown out of that stage. Why does that have to be? I'll tell you right now that if you can become mesmerized by your own ideas and goals, you will achieve them faster than if you sit there and contemplate why your ideas and goals cannot be achieved.

## CHAPTER 34

# LET YOUR LITTLE CHILD OUT EVERY ONCE IN A WHILE

Let your little child out every once in a while. Nobody has to know except you. Remember, I didn't say act like a child, I said think like a child. Look at Elon Musk. That guy probably lets his inner child out every day and look what he has done, not to mention the fact that he is laughing all the way to the bank.

Getting back to trying and figure out what others are thinking, it is not only a waste of time but it is an endless road to nowhere. Thinking of yourself is the easiest way to explain it. How many times a week do you change how you feel about certain things? Could anyone know for sure that you vacillated on these things and changed your mind? Not unless you took out a bullhorn and made an announcement in the streets. Although not a pleasant thing to discuss, I'm going to give you a valid example of how your thoughts can change from one second to the next. So here goes: What would you do if a gun was pointed at you? There is really only one answer to that question and that is that you don't know. You really don't. It all depends on what is going on in your mind at that very second. I understand that your life is in danger 'and I'm not disputing that fact for one single second. However, if at that very second you think you're going to be abducted, you might fight as opposed to surrendering. Your reaction in a situation like that could be different from one minute to the next. My point is that even if you might be right about what someone is thinking, they can change their mind ten minutes from now.

The bottom line is to live your life with the best intentions for everyone and everything. Don't put words in people's mouths. Don't make assumptions. Go forward and believe that all things will work out. My other piece of advice is that there doesn't have to be a right or a wrong to everything. Value other opinions. Don't shut others down. You yourself would want others to value your opinions so value theirs. There will always be disagreements but you can always compromise as well.

## CHAPTER 35

# LEARN NEW THINGS

You can also learn so many new things when you allow others to voice their opinions. Your current core beliefs just might be enlightened by someone you least expect by allowing new possibilities and thoughts into your life. Along the same lines, don't cut people off when they are talking to you. What I mean by that has nothing to do with being rude. It's just that you may inadvertently interrupt because you don't want to forget what you're about to say. I understand that and I wish I had a dollar for every time I did that. However, you really need to restrain yourself from interrupting someone because they can very easily misconstrue your intentions by thinking that you are indeed being rude. Hold on to the thought that you might forget. If it were that important, it will come up in conversation over the next few minutes. You could always keep a tiny notepad in your hand and write down your thought that you will forget although that is probably not advisable.

One last thing when conversing with others. This occurred about fifteen years ago and I've never forgotten it. I'm actually happy that it did occur. There was a fellow gym member that was always near my locker. We would talk when we saw each other and he was a very nice guy.

However, I truly believe that he never really heard a thing that I said because he was just talking but never listening. I remember one particular time when we were talking about a famous athlete. I had actually met this athlete and proceeded to try and tell him about it. He didn't even hear me when I told him that I met the guy! It was incredible. My main point here is that you will never learn anything new if you don't listen.

On the flip side, my ex business partner and I went to meet one of the major gas station owners in New York. He had multiple gas stations branded with his own logo and he had an excellent reputation. We were thinking of possibly selling our much smaller operation to him. We were with him for over an hour. When we left, we realized that he barely spoke at all. All he was doing was gathering information that the both of us talked about nonstop for an hour. He received all the information he wanted and we ended up with no information at all. We never made a deal but we learned a great deal. We did the talking and he did the learning.

## CHAPTER 36

# PRACTICE SPONTANEITY

It is time to discuss spontaneity. Most of us live mundane lives. It is mainly because we have an inordinate amount of things that need to be done on a daily basis. We have jobs that require us to be working from 9-5 Monday through Friday. We have to keep food in the house. A lot of us have young children that need to be attended to. Despite the fact that I work from home, I am still running errands at least three to four times a week. And how many phone calls do we receive every day? How many text messages and emails do we have to always deal with?

You get my point. So where and when do we have the time to be spontaneous? It really is a simple answer. When you get a request to do something out of the ordinary, you say yes. I'm not saying that you say yes every time. I'm saying that you say yes sometimes. You'll be amazed at how refreshing it feels when you do. It will allow you to tackle the mundane things in a whole new way. I have started saying yes and my life has changed for the better. I even welcome things from out of the ordinary now instead of getting upset that I have to change my every day routine.

## CHAPTER 37

# RELATIONSHIPS

I knew a couple who made sure that they took one night a month to go to a hotel to keep the excitement in their marriage. They even went out of their way to do it during the week and on a different day of the week every time.

On that note, that is just one way, (and a great way) to keep things flourishing in a relationship. When either partner is feeling down in the dumps, it puts a strain on both of you. What I'm getting at here is that there is no more important facet of a partnership or relationship than communication. It is literally the key to keeping your relationship strong and secure. So, when either one is struggling with a problem, it is essential to at least try and figure out what needs to be solved together. If that is not possible in a particular problem, both of you need to at least discuss the fact that you need your partner to at least know that you need to tackle this one yourself. Your partner will at least know that they will be there to support you when you feel comfortable enough to address it with them.

This exact problem happened to a very close friend of mine and his relationship ended because of it. The woman he was dating had some sort of physical problem that he was clueless about. He kept asking her what was wrong and she would not clue him in. I think that it is important to point out that he had not become intimate yet and being intimate had not even been discussed in any way. He never pressured her to tell him what was wrong. All he said was this: I'm not asking you to tell me what is wrong. All I'm asking you to tell me is whether or not there is any sort of problem. She never did tell him if she had some sort of problem. He found out from a mutual friend that she was being operated on for a minor procedure. How do you develop a trusting relationship if someone will not at least be fair enough to mention that there is indeed a problem but that he or she does not want to discuss what it is at this time?

He eventually lost interest in pursuing a relationship with her because she didn't feel that it was important enough to tell him that she had some sort of problem. There had been no pressure on his part whatsoever to take the relationship to the next level.

As you can easily see in this example, communication was absent from this relationship. When you don't say what is on your mind on a continuous basis, your relationship is ultimately doomed. This doesn't mean that you have a right to be nasty but you do have every right to voice your opinion (being good or bad) and not feel that you're going to be challenged with everything you say. I believe that a good back and forth discussion can strengthen a relationship as opposed to hurting it.

I'm not saying that you should be argumentative but what I am saying is that if you hold everything in all the time you will end up very resentful and your relationship will begin to disintegrate. Be as honest as you can with your partner. If you're not, your partner will start to doubt your willingness to be truthful. And if an argument does come to the surface, make sure to watch your words. You don't want to say something in anger that you might regret.

Also remember that when you apologize, it strengthens the relationship.

One of the best ways to show your partner that you care about them is by complimenting them on what you appreciate about them. Keep your criticism to a minimum. Harp on the good things. Always remember why you were initially attracted to them. Make sure to spend quality time with them. Pay attention when they speak to you. Let them know that you really and truly care. Make time for one on one encounters and I'm not just talking about the physical encounters. It is all the other types of encounters that lead up to the great physical ones.

Go to dinner. Send loving text messages. Leave notes by the night table. Tell them how great they make you feel and how happy you are that you're with them. Most importantly, do all these things when the kids are not around. You can do these little things even if the kids are around. Just don't involve them. Make sure your partner is the only one you're thinking of at that moment. If you feel guilty about leaving the kids out of it, go into their rooms afterward and tell them how much you love them.

There are so many powerful and positive words in the English language. Love is one of them. Being in love is an emotion that can drive you to be at the very height of your capabilities. I'm not only talking about being in love with your significant other. It can be a goal you're about to achieve, it could be a new pet that you just brought into your home. It could even be your job.

## CHAPTER 38

# YOUR MONEY STORY

Napoleon Hill wrote one of the most famous books ever written called Think and Grow Rich. The book is not only about making money. In it, he mentions the fact that when two people are in love, they climb to a different atmosphere, one that makes them unstoppable.

Other words that come to mind are happy, terrific, wonderful, and great. I couldn't list them all even if I wanted to but you get my point. Do you think that you can feel bad if you use any of these words? It would be almost impossible. This is why you need to watch your words. Harp on the positive ones and use the negative ones sparingly. For instance, there are five words that I have recently taken out of my vocabulary. They are worry, overwhelm, failure, lack, and poverty. Do you think that you can feel good by using these particular words? Once again, I highly doubt it. You might be curious as to why I chose those five particular words. Let me explain.

**Worry.** It does absolutely nothing whatsoever. You need to take some sort of action when it comes to worry.

**Overwhelm.** Make a list of what you're overwhelmed about and take care of the toughest thing on the list first. The rest of the list will no longer be overwhelming.

**Failure.** There is no such thing. The only time you can fail is when you give up. Here is a great example. Do you think it's possible to start a new business without any problems? It is literally impossible. Am I wrong here? I don't think so.

**Lack.** If you think lack, that is exactly what you're going to get. Always think abundance. We are all entitled to abundance. The more you have, the more people you can help.

**Poverty.** Same goes here. Get wealthy and show poverty stricken people how to acquire wealth. You will feel better than just saying you feel sorry for them.

It is the right of everyone to be rich. As a matter of fact, if you want to help the world to be a better place, it is your obligation to become wealthy. Yes, that's right. I said it. When I first read that, I was flabbergasted. But after I thought about it, it really made sense to me. Think of it this way: It might just be what you need to catapult you to the next level. A statement of this magnitude, can take a thought such as, I don't deserve to be rich and blow that negative thought right out of your mind. I actually think that whoever came up with that line deserves the highest of praise.

When it is said that it is your obligation to become rich, it reminds me of the guy that came up on stage and started to kiss the cash that he had in his hand. Remember how horrified the audience was when he did that? These negative thoughts that we have about money need to be eradicated more sooner than later. You have to sit down and take a very long look as to what your money story is. We all have one and it doesn't matter as to whether or not you have ten dollars or millions of dollars.

Our money stories have been deep rooted in our minds from a very young age. How do you handle the money that you have? What does money really mean to you? If you want to accumulate more of it, you need to become aware of the fact that you really do deserve it. Remember the story about the guy who was only able to make thirty thousand dollars a year and now consistently makes seven figures? Do yourself a favor and do whatever it takes to change your money story from *Money Is The Root Of All Evil to Money Is A Great Gift That I Can Share With The World* or use your own set of words to switch out the bad beliefs and replace them with good beliefs.

If your money story came from your parents, you must remember that they were only trying to keep you safe. Most of those beliefs are antiquated and come from ideas that were put into their heads from your grandparents. For those of us who are in our fifties and sixties, do you not truly believe that some of these thoughts are no longer useful?

If you're struggling with changing around your money story, it is vital that you begin immediately to reprogram your subconscious mind through positive affirmations that need to be said out loud at least two to three times a day. Write them down on a sheet of paper and use emotion when you say them. This has to be done every single day. The best times are when you first wake up and right before you go to sleep.

Our money stories are deep rooted and will not go away easily. They got into your subconscious at a very young age and have stayed there all this time. Are you a saver or a spender? Do you pay your bills on time? Do you have a good credit score?

The reason I bring this up is because most of us have very convoluted ideas when it comes to money. Some of the richest people in the world are very poor tippers. Some people (like me) are penny wise and dollar foolish. Some very poor people throw money around as if they have millions. And here is the best money story of all. A very, very high percentage of lottery winners lose ALL their money in a very short period of time.

Now that we have discussed our money story, what is it that we need to do to get in the frame of mind to be able to change our negative thoughts when it comes to money or any other thing that is currently holding us back from succeeding? First of all, you must make a concerted effort to go through all the things you do on a daily basis and how you go about doing them. How many hours a day are you wasting by talking about your problems? How many news shows do you watch that delve into negative issues?

You need to weed out the negativity in your life and replace it with positivity. You'll never be able to change your money story or anything else in your life until you change your mindset. We all have people in our life that bring us down. They are detrimental to our wellbeing. If you can't get them completely out of your life, at least cut the time that you spend with them significantly. Maybe you can help change them to your way of thinking. Don't count on that though. Read positivity books. Watch educational shows. Read your affirmations every day. You will see that your life will begin to change and you'll have more abundance.

## CHAPTER 39

# HOW WE VIEW OUR LOVED ONES

It's time to take a look at how we view our loved ones. You should only have the best of intentions when it comes to your loved ones. Unfortunately, things can get in the way and there are many times when these things can be avoided if you knew what really caused them. For instance, let's use your spouse or significant other as a good example. You are going through a rough stretch. Things are not going well at work and you're continually frustrated. You take your frustration home with you day after day. You come home and you see your significant other. You would never stop to realize that your troubled demeanor is beginning to include him or her, yet they have absolutely nothing to do with the problem. However, the two things have now been subconsciously linked up and though unaware, you start unknowingly treating your significant other poorly. This can lead to unfortunate circumstances and you wouldn't even be aware that it is happening.

You can also see how this same sort of thing can happen with your parents. This is a much deeper rooted problem and once again, there is a good chance that you might not be aware of what is going on. As these unfortunate situations occur in your life, you may start blaming your parents because it is so much easier to do than to blame yourself or the actual event or events that are causing you to feel bad. If only my mother had not said this or if only my father had done this than I would not be having this problem right now.

This can expand into blaming siblings, or friends as well. Remember our minds are simply trying to protect ourselves from harm. In most cases, we are not consciously aware that we are blaming others for our trials and tribulations. We are simply trying to protect ourselves from pain and hurt. Your subconscious mind will do whatever it has to keep you safe. But unless you start to become aware of what you're doing, you might (and probably will) be alienating your loved ones. You really don't want to do that. You don't want to lose a loved one or loved ones over something that they really have nothing to do with.

Texting is another great example of how you can lose someone close to you. Although texting is a quick and easy way to communicate, it can be dangerous when said text is totally misunderstood. I think we would all agree that there are thousands of people out there at this very moment who are angry over a text that they received, that was entirely misunderstood. When I text someone, I always reread it. If I think that there is the slightest chance that the text could have more than one meaning, I'll change it by stating what I did mean as opposed to what the other person might think I meant. The other problem with texting is making sure the text is going to the right person. Make sure to keep your texts positive so that if you accidentally send it to the wrong person, it is no big deal.

Look to improve every day. Challenge yourself when you wake up by saying out loud that you are going to win the day and do whatever it takes every single day to make sure that you're constantly improving. Obviously, this is not an easy task. But as you start to stack these days one after the other, you will not want to disappoint yourself by falling back.

I'm fully aware that you can only keep this up to a certain point, so get through as many days as you can. When the streak has ended, begin a new one and outdo the one you just finished. Think of the marathon runner. Do you think he or she woke up one morning and just ran twenty miles. No way. They ran from their house for a block or so. The next day, they ran fifty or one hundred yards more and so on and so on until the day came that they were able to run twenty miles or more. How about the weight lifter? Do you think they lifted two hundred pounds the very first time they tried. Of course not. Everything occurs in increments.

You can apply this formula to just about anything in life. Relationships are another very good example. Does a man ask a woman to marry him in the first five minutes on their very first date? Does he or she reveal everything about themselves right away? Trust is built up over a period of time and I mean trusting yourself as well. Can I win the day every day? Can I run that extra half a mile today? Can I lift five more pounds today? Can I reveal more about myself on the next date? Do I feel that I can really trust this new person in my life? You will never know unless you try. Trust yourself to know the answer to these questions.

## CHAPTER 40

# THINK LIKE A WINNER

Think like a winner. You know right from wrong. Trust yourself to do the right thing. Have the courage to proceed in spite of fear and anxiety. Think more of your strengths than your weaknesses.

The most important thing as you expand your horizons is to not be afraid of your emotions. It is totally normal to feel nervous or apprehensive as you embark on these new paths. We are all human beings. You can't help from being nervous. Famous actors and athletes still get nervous before they get up to perform.

I will use myself as an example and no, I am not a famous actor or athlete. I am taking being nervous in stride because I am telling myself the following before I get up in front of a large group of people: I want to help others so badly, that I will be doing all of them a disservice if I don't get up there and do this and even if it doesn't go perfectly, there is always next time and I will improve each and every time I do it. I also say to myself that when Tony Robbins was to do his very first program, he invited approximately one hundred people and only two people showed up. If he can persevere, so can I.

There is no way to fight the stage fright so you are better

off to embrace it. Once again, you must remember that you are a human being who is not a robot. Nor do you want to be a robot. Speak with passion. Go after what you want with passion. Let everyone see how much you really care. Especially yourself.

Speak kindly to yourself. This is extremely important. I know that you are your biggest critic. We all are. But you must lighten up. You are not perfect my friend and will never be. For me, that is such a wonderful revelation. Just think, if you were, life would be the epitome of boring. What is there to live for if you're perfect.

There is always something to learn. There is always something new to do. There are also new ways to do the same things that you are doing now. Think of all the new people that you are bound to meet in the coming months. Harp on the wonderful new adventures that are about to come your way. Striving to be perfect is an endless road to nowhere. Ease up on yourself. If you make a mistake, learn from it as opposed to beating yourself up. If you accidentally say something harsh to a loved one, friend, or coworker, swallow your pride and tell them that you're sorry. Otherwise, the mistake will fester and balloon into an unnecessary problem, especially if you're the one that made the mistake.

Go forward with the best of intentions. Continue to learn how to turn around the difficult things in your life. Don't be afraid to fail because there is no such thing as failure. Failure is simply feedback. Now you know what not to do and begin to do what you need to do.

Don't worry about anything. The actual act of worry does absolutely nothing. All you can do with worry is take action. Don't think lack or poverty, think abundance. Never just try. Do it. Trying is giving you the option to fail. Don't allow these words to stay in your vocabulary.

Think like a winner. Only talk about your wins. Forget about your losses. We all have losses but we don't need to dwell on them. Losses are there to help teach us how to win. That is why there is no such thing as failure. Failure is only feedback. It is there to show you what doesn't work which brings you that much closer to what does work. Utilize all your losses and failures. Learn from them so you'll be that much closer to wins and success in your life.

The more you keep your mind in tune with winning, the farther you'll be away from losing. As I keep saying, we are what we think about.

I saw a short film a few years back as to how powerful the mind can be. It's about a particular player on a High School football team. They were on the field about to practice and the coach began to discuss their next opponent who were undefeated. The same player that I just referenced raised his hand and told the coach that there was no way that they could beat this undefeated team. The coach then had this player come to the end zone and told him to get down on his hands and knees. The coach then blindfolded the player. He then called another player over and had him get on the blindfolded player's back.

Coach then asked the blindfolded player if he could crawl on his knees for ten yards with the other player on his back. He said: I'll do my best coach. The blindfolded player began his quest for the ten yards with the other player and the coach cheering him on. The coach encouraged him to keep going and he'll soon make the ten yards.

The coach started to chant words of encouragement to the player. He kept asking him if he could make it. He challenged the player over and over and needless to say, the final result was nothing short of astonishing. When the player collapsed and subsequently removed the blindfold, he had traveled the entire length of the football field with the other player still on his back. The following Saturday, they beat the undefeated team.

You can never imagine what heights you can reach if you give yourself the chance to succeed. If you can believe it, you can achieve it. Begin to believe in yourself more and more. Leave all the naysayers behind. You need to know that you can and will accomplish all your goals.

Your goal achieving is contingent upon believing that you will. Do you believe that you will achieve your physical goals? Most of us have no reason to believe that we won't. Why? Because they are not as psychologically driven as other goals. You can readily envision putting five more pounds on the bar and lifting it up. You also know that even though your muscles will be sore, the soreness will dissipate in a day or so. So why don't we treat our mentally driven goals the same? It is because of our early childhood beliefs.

I know that it makes no sense that we are mature adults now but it does make sense when we realize that these childhood beliefs are buried in our subconscious minds and although we are full grown adults, these ideas and thoughts are holding us back from getting what we want.

Your subconscious mind will fight you tooth and nail for what was planted in it so many years ago. You have to fight back with everything you have to form new beliefs and eradicate the old unwanted ones. Your subconscious mind has no capacity whatsoever to determine right from wrong. It believes whatever you put into it or tell it. Therefore, you have got to reprogram your subconscious mind by using positive affirmations, and saying them out loud at least a few times per day. It CAN be done, but it will not happen overnight.

Read books that go against your old beliefs. Be cognizant of what your negative beliefs are telling you. Remember the fact that your subconscious mind will fight you to keep you from changing the old beliefs. Make sure that your affirmations are the direct opposite of those old school limiting beliefs.

This is 2021. It is not 1965. What your parents planted in your brain in 1965 is no longer applicable in 2021. And you must also remember that your parents' job was to keep you safe. They were doing nothing wrong. But now is the time to take full control of your life.

For those of you who think that your beliefs can be changed at the drop of a hat, I'd like to cite two examples from my own life and these two things I'm totally aware of. First of all, I never go to the movies without bringing a jacket with me and I don't care if it is 90 degrees outside. This is because when I was about ten years old, my Dad took me to a movie where I was wearing shorts and a tee shirt. We had to leave because I started to cry. That's how cold I was and that was within the first half hour of the movie. The second example is my total dislike of egg salad. I like eggs and I like mayonnaise but I can't even stand the smell of egg salad. This is all because I got sick from egg salad when I was around seven years old and I still can't get past it.

After citing those two examples of things that I'm actually aware of and can't get past, imagine how crazy I might get for things that I have absolutely no idea about. This goes for all of us. Everyone is guilty of this. We all have our idiosyncrasies and I can assure you that most of them are caused by our early childhood beliefs.

Add the relationship factor onto all these idiosyncratic behaviors. Can you imagine how many divorces have occurred because someone could no longer handle their partner's idiosyncrasies? At least begin to work on the ones you're aware of while having some patience and compassion for the idiosyncrasies of your partner.

I have slowly modified my jacket and egg salad thoughts

over the last few weeks. I started wearing an extra shirt instead of bringing a jacket into a movie., and I actually tasted some egg salad in the last two or three months although it is definitely not my favorite.

We all must do our best to handle the beliefs that are stopping us from growing. When we have an idea that might change our life for the better, we tend to put this great idea off to the side, doubting that this or any other idea may or may not work right now or may not come to fruition. What is really going on here, is that that we're frightened because it is not the norm. We have been thrust out of our comfort zone by this new idea. We don't have enough confidence to believe that said idea can actually come to fruition.

We are all creatures of habit and even the mere thought of coming out of our comfort zone can scare us right out of our shoes. Think of it this way. Have you ever heard of someone who has stopped smoking or stopped drinking without actually knowing that they just have to? Why would anyone give up either of these so called pleasurable habits unless they knew it was bad for them? We have to do this with all of our outdated beliefs in the same way as we would to acknowledge that smoking and excess drinking are insidious to your everyday health.

We are what we think about. This is why I preach abundance and not allow lack and poverty into my thoughts. Every single one of us is entitled to abundance. The more abundance you have, the more people you can help as long as you do it constructively, and creatively. It is not to be done competitively. The more people you help; the more help will come to you. It is the natural chain of events.

Never give though, in lieu of receiving anything back. Never give a gift if you expect something back. It is only a gift when you don't expect anything back. However, you will always get back something in return. It just may not necessarily be from the one you gave it to.

There are so many people who can't handle any sort of change. They go through the same routine day after day after day. Then the weekend comes and although things might be a bit different, the weekend also becomes the same weekend after weekend.

Taking it to an even deeper extreme, some people live in the same house their whole lives not because they can't afford to move but simply because they can't handle any sort of change. I personally know three examples of this. In the first one, my parents sold their house to a religious couple in Brooklyn. They are still there and that transaction took place in 1963. In the second example, the following story happened in Queens, N.Y.: A very huge mall was being built and all the home owners in this area were bought out by the conglomerate behind the mall. However, there was one stubborn woman who simply would not move. She was offered way more than all the other home owners received. End result was that the mall was built around this ladies' house. If you are ever on Queens Boulevard, feel free to check it out.

The final example is the wife of a former business associate of mine. Our business was doing well and it was going to allow this associate to move from a very small apartment, to a big and beautiful house. The house was less than five minutes from the apartment but the wife could not handle it at first. They were able to keep the same telephone number and she could still shop at the same exact stores that she was used to. They came within a whisker of getting divorced. It is unimaginable as to how many people can't handle any sort of change, even when the change is definitively for the better.

This is why we have to process our thoughts on a daily

basis. We need to be able to decipher as to what is good and what is bad as well as what is right and what is wrong. I don't mean to imply that we will always know right from wrong but we need to at least try to be on the right side of the equation more times than not.

Don't be so quick to judge the motives of others. You have to be trusting sometimes that others have your best interest at heart. That includes being too sensitive. Would you rather not have someone tell you when you're at fault? You'll never, ever improve if somebody just yesses you all the time. When you're overly sensitive, you run the risk of alienating those around you. They are not going to feel free enough to let you know what they really think. Instead, they are only going to tell you want you want to hear. Is that really what you want? I wouldn't think so.

Watch your words and watch your thoughts. Take the time to think before you speak. You don't want to say something that you might regret. Take a deep breath before you let loose with a tirade. Make believe you are a famous person whose every word is being monitored for print. Only send out emails that you know will not upset someone or be misconstrued.

Look for the good in everyone. When you do, you will rarely (if ever) have to watch your words. I fully understand that you can't like everyone. However, there is something in everyone that will help you connect to the good and to weed out what only seems like all bad. Look at it from this perspective: There are certain things about YOU that might not be looked at in the best of ways. None of us are perfect and although you cannot fathom how somebody wouldn't like you, believe it or not when I say that there is something about each and every one of us that someone else might not tend to like.

I have opinions on just about everything and I like to

voice these opinions. I pride myself in allowing others to voice theirs but if someone vehemently objects to one of mine, there is an excellent chance that they are not going to like me. A long time ago, I gave up in trying to get every single person in the world to like me. Unless you mute yourself on every single topic, there is going to be others who don't like your particular opinion on the topic being discussed. And guess what? Even those who do mute themselves on all their opinions are not going to be liked because they will be viewed as stuffed shirts for not speaking up.

## CHAPTER 41

# JUST BE YOURSELF

The bottom line is to just be yourself, be courteous to all and see the good in everyone as opposed to certain things you don't like. Sometimes, you just might catch a person who just had a rough day. Is it fair to wrongly judge a person who just had a bad day? Think twice before you go off on a tangent on what a nasty person you just met.

A great example of this is road rage. A good percentage of the time, the driver of another car is angry with someone else and is taking it out on you because he or she doesn't want to confront the person that they are angry with. How many times in all the years that you've been driving have you cursed at someone or have had someone curse at you? Hopefully these incidents occurred with your windows closed. But my point is that you are not the only one doing the cursing. Nobody is the perfect driver. We all make mistakes. Learn to let it go. You're not the only one who is trying to get to work or to get home.

By thinking fondly of others, it will put you in the positive cycle and distance you from the negative cycle. This is the best way to turn your life into constant joy. You're always going to run into people who rub you the wrong way, get under your skin or just plain irritate you.

Simply talk silently to yourself and say whatever you need to say to avoid a stare down, or even frown at someone else. Remember that you have done some things yourself that can upset someone. When you train yourself to always think fondly of others, you will attract so many nicer people into your life and these new people can end up being close friends of yours. You would never have attracted these new people if you're always walking around looking as if you're angry with the world.

Smile at strangers that you see when you are out and about. I bet you that most will smile back. This will give you an opportunity to engage in conversation if you so choose. When two people smile at each other, that means that either one of them is more than likely to be approachable. You might be the one that can change their life and/or they could be the one to change your life. It is a very small world. Everyone knows someone that is looking for help with all kinds of endeavors.

You never know what someone is thinking so don't let that deter you from engaging someone in conversation. It is such a small world and the next person you meet could be a springboard for you to change the timing of your goal from six months to six days just because you met him or her.

I could write this book strictly on my own personal small world stories. Here is the wildest one. I was a member of a Singles company looking for my better half. They sent me to Manhattan to meet her. I was living on Long Island at the time. She mentioned that she only knew one person who lived on Long Island. It turned out that this Uncle of hers was somebody I've known since I could walk or talk and his son is still one of my closest friends. It also turned out that her father and his mother were siblings. That is not the end of the story. Four days later, this same company had me meet another woman at a restaurant on

Long Island. Turns out that she went to law school with another close friend and his wife. What are the odds of that?

In case anyone might be interested, they were both very nice but neither one of them were a match for me. Maybe in those days, I was looking for Miss Perfect. I realized soon after that Mr. Perfect and/or Miss Perfect do not exist.

All of these small world experiences, have led me to believe that you never know how or when a particular person is going to come into your life and turn your world upside down. I don't only mean a possible love relationship. It could mean a business relationship of some sort. I can tell you this: It is not only me when it comes to small world stories. I know a man who ran into his Long Island next door neighbor at a Dodgers game in Los Angeles. I know a woman who ran into a couple in London that knew her grandmother. So remember to keep your eyes and ears open at all times. I know this. If I was in Singapore tomorrow and ran into my neighbor, I would simply say Hi there Jim. HI there Barbara. Nice to see you. See you next week when we're home.

Always remember that unless you go forward, you're staying the same. This is not what you want is it? Better yet, isn't it time to step out of your comfort zone? I've been brave enough over the last year to step out of my comfort zone. Why? Because I gave myself a great reason to do so. I began to think and more importantly feel that I am now at the point that I'm here to help as many people as I can. If I don't do this, I'm doing a disservice to all the people that can use my help. There are so many people that I can help and I have to do it. More importantly, I want to do it, so I am.

I'm writing this book as well as doing daily videos online that I'm getting compliments and thanks on every single day. I'm also speaking to groups about changing their negative beliefs to positive ones. Another reason that I'm doing this is that I have a brother that is multi-talented and my Mom was the same. Neither did anything with their extraordinary talent and it was such a shame. My mother could have been an opera star and that is no exaggeration whatsoever. My brother is a multitalented musician who sounds exactly like Don Henley, has written at least twenty great songs and is an expert drummer and guitarist. He also never did anything with his talent.

You must do something with your God given talent. I worked in the gas station business for thirty years and in the hair salon business for twenty years. I had no love for either job but I learned what I had to learn, did very well and never, ever thought to do something that I loved. COVID changed all that. When COVID hit and I was let go from my Salon Job as an area manager, I had two choices. One was to sit in the corner and cry in the fetal position all day and the other choice was to do something that would make me happy for the very first time.

I sat down and asked myself the following question: What do you love to do? What are your passions? I came up with the two answers rather quickly. First of all, I love to help people. I get a tremendous feeling of accomplishment when I've helped someone. And the second one is my love of sports. As a result, I'm writing this book, doing daily videos, and doing weekly sportscasts with a partner. I'm not going to tell you to heed my advice right away but I am going to tell you to start contemplating a move in the near future to a job that would make you much happier than the way you might feel right now.

For those of you that are retired, start doing something on an everyday basis that makes you want to jump out of bed every morning. Be inspired on a daily basis. Don't be bored every day.

## CHAPTER 42
# SOME GREAT QUOTES

Time for some great quotes that I'd like to share:

*"All of our dreams can come true if we have the courage to pursue them."* – WALT DISNEY.

*"The future belongs to those who believe in the beauty of their dreams."* – ELEANOR ROOSEVELT.

*"Busy your mind with concepts of harmony, health, peace, and good will and wonders will happen in your life."* – DR. JOSEPH MURPHY

*"Stick to your purpose, retain your vision, and maintain your faith and gratitude."* – WALLACE WATTLES.

And my favorite by DR. NORMAN VINCENT PEALE: *"If it is to be it is up to me."*

Always read books about positivity and write your positive affirmations every day. Read them out loud. When you do these things on a consistent basis, you will find that your whole life will begin to change. You will appreciate what you have so much more. You will welcome new and beautiful things into your life, you will attract new, positive people and most importantly, you will begin to see how wonderful this life of ours really is and always should be.

When you read these inspiring thoughts, how does it make you feel? I made it a point to pick very influential people who are looked up to for various reasons. All these quotes were made so you would think deeply about where you are right now and where you are headed. Your mindset needs to be on the right frequency in order to attract the type of people that will help bring you to the next level.

## CHAPTER 43

# MINDSET IS EVERYTHING

Mindset is everything. As I've said before, we are what we think about. Words like overwhelm, worry, failure, lack, poverty, and try need to be replaced by words such as calm, action, feedback, abundance, riches, and will. There is no need to feel overwhelmed. Take a deep breath and remain **CALM** when you start to feel overwhelmed. Make a list and simply do the things that need to be done, one by one until the feeling of overwhelm is gone. Failure is simply **FEEDBACK**. Now you know what doesn't work so find something else that does. The actual act of worry does absolutely nothing. You must take **ACTION** to combat worry. **ABUNDANCE** is certainly better than lack. Train your brain to welcome abundance into your life and send lack packing. Never talk poverty again. Search out **RICHES** and make poverty go away forever. Don't ever say that you'll try. Try, screams of a losing attitude. Instead use **WILL** in whatever you're after. I **WILL** achieve what I'm after, I won't just try. Trying is not an option.

Using positive words as opposed to negative ones will help bring you into the money frequency and allow you to further believe in abundance. There are so many people who believe that money is the root of all evil and it is selfish and so wrong to want abundance. Why is that? It is because as we're growing up, our subconscious minds are being filled with things that are just not true. Have you ever heard those who say, I just want to have enough to be able to pay my bills and go on a nice vacation every couple of years or so?

I used to believe these comments wholeheartedly but they should no longer be believed. Remember the guy on stage who was kissing money and who left the audience aghast? I can guarantee you that even to this day, virtually everyone in that audience would be so upset with that guy. How dare he be up there kissing money.

Everyone should be applauding this guy because he is trying to teach us how important it is to have money and how we are all entitled to as much abundance as we can possibly accumulate. It is also important to mention that I'm talking about those who are looking to do the proper things with the money that they accumulate.

Teach those who are living in poverty as to how they can become independent and abundant. Help them to change their thoughts about wealth, independence, and abundance. Look to constantly improve. Buy the expensive car, go on a luxurious vacation, move to a nicer house.

Don't be afraid to succeed. You deserve the opportunity to show the world what you've got. Think how great you would feel to be financially free and to know that you can help families that are in need. How about being in the forefront of an idea that can change the world? You could be the next Elon Musk or Thomas Edison. You would then have fame and fortune. All these things are in our grasp. If you believe, you can achieve.

Of course there is no need to become famous but there is a need for more millionaires and billionaires who will hopefully help those that are unfortunate. These new rich people could show the poverty stricken, ways to change their misfortunes into fortunes. There is never a better time to show everyone a better way than right now.

There are so many people suffering from depression. Lack of sympathy and lack of affection are the primary causes of depression. Don't be afraid to tell a friend that you love them. This can go a long way to defeating depression. Stay away from negative literature, shoot 'em up movies, and the late night newscasts.

It is time to realize, that if you change your way of thinking even just a little bit per day, you can improve your life tenfold. Take out a piece of paper and write out what you do every day. Are you thinking positively when you're doing these things? Are you just going through the motions like a robot? Are you just counting down the hours and minutes till you get to the weekend? Do you dread going to sleep on Sunday night because you know that when you wake up, it is Monday morning and you have to go through that vicious cycle of Monday through Friday?

I felt the same exact way for many years. I know now that life is not meant to be like that. It is time to figure out a better way. You need to start to climb out of the abyss and I say abyss because that's what it seems like sometimes or maybe all the time.

Do not make any irrational decisions but start planning an alternative. Don't do what I did by staying in a business that doesn't suit you. I did that twice and I even did well but it left me unsatisfied so for the first time, I'm doing something that I truly love and I'm happy.

Begin to vastly improve what you do right now but begin to think what would really make you happy and it can come to fruition if you really want it. But it is imperative that you work harder in what you're doing right now so that you'll be in the right frame of mind when it comes to pass for you to make the necessary change. You know what would really jazz you so start thinking that way and before you know it, you can be making money at what you love. This will most likely not happen overnight and could actually take quite a while but if you acquire the right mindset and work harder at what you are presently doing it will happen in due time.

Whether you improve right away or not, you have to keep the faith that you will figure out whatever you need to figure out. This could be a small problem that needs to be fixed in your house or a financial problem that needs to be immediately addressed. It can be your current relationship with a loved one, sibling, parent or business associate. Just know that you can figure out anything as long as you put your mind to it. This will allow you to grow. Otherwise, you stay in the safety zone, a zone where one never takes a chance and would rather stay status quo.

We are all here to learn and to grow and to experience new things. Take a chance and get out of your comfort zone. I'm not saying by any stretch of the imagination that that will be easy but if we're all totally honest with ourselves, it sure beats doing the same thing day after day and week after week. As I've said before, try a new restaurant, or take a drive to a brand new place.

If you are in a relationship, discuss ideas as to where you can both go on your next vacation. Make a list together of new places to explore. Visit a museum, go to a winery or an art gallery even if you have little interest in the three things I just mentioned. Have fun with this. Make sure that neither one of you ever did something like this before.

One thing you don't want to do is to get into an argument as to what you would like to do which brings me to another important topic and that is being careful when you get angry. Take a deep breath and a brief pause before you say something that you will most likely regret. No matter what it is, you will be better off in the long run. The angrier you are, the more likely you are to say something that is really hurtful. There have been many times in my life where I held back confronting someone about something and in every single case, I'm glad I did.

Two other things on this subject. You will find that many times, you would be telling someone off for no reason because you misunderstood what they were trying to say and the other thing is that when you are upset with someone, make sure that you discuss your disagreement in private. Don't ever air dirty laundry in public. That is not fair to anyone involved including you. I learned from my Dad and his side of the family. They all constantly screamed at each other and could care less as to who was around when they were so rude to everyone around them.

Sit down with pad and paper and write out a plan on how you would like to proceed in any and all of your endeavors. Be very specific and list things in order of their importance. Take things one by one and start to implement them. Never take on more than one or two things at a time. Go about your plan slowly but surely. Ask for help from people that you trust. Make sure that the person or persons that you're asking help from is not out to sabotage you. This is very important. As I've said before in my example of losing weight, your confidant might not even know that they're sabotaging you. Deep in their subconscious mind, they don't want you to change too much so they unknowingly may try to hold you back from attaining your goal.

It is also important to note that you can employ numerous people as your confidants. Just make sure to use the right person for the right reasons. As it is with everything in life, one confidant or many confidants could work in your favor or cannot work in your favor. If you have numerous ones, don't share all your needs and wants with all of them. Just employ one or two with each problem, or task that you are trying to accomplish.

As you continue to progress, you must be persistent. Go after what you want and don't let up until you achieve your goal. The time is now. Yesterday is gone. Tomorrow is not here as of yet. Stop putting things off. Get rid of all the excuses. Procrastination is no longer an option. Think back to the story of Sylvester Stallone. He gave up everything in order to pursue his dream. He sold his wife's jewelry. He sold his dog. He turned down a deal that was offered him in which Rocky was going to be played by Ryan O'Neal. He insisted that he was Rocky. He never gave up despite the fact that he was turned down for his Rocky script by all of the directors he tried, some of which turned him down numerous times.

Write down statements for yourself along the lines of what Sylvester Stallone had to do in order to get Rocky to be filmed with him as the star. I'm sure that none of us can even imagine what Stallone went through in order to persevere. Read your statements out loud a number of times per day until you start to really believe them. At first you will have your doubts but with the passing of each and every day, you will know that you can get this done. Your positive words will begin to take effect.